1 MONTH OF
FREE
READING

at
www.ForgottenBooks.com

By purchasing this book you are eligible for one month membership to ForgottenBooks.com, giving you unlimited access to our entire collection of over 700,000 titles via our web site and mobile apps.

To claim your free month visit:
www.forgottenbooks.com/free731683

* Offer is valid for 45 days from date of purchase. Terms and conditions apply.

ISBN 978-0-484-14369-1
PIBN 10731683

This book is a reproduction of an important historical work. Forgotten Books uses state-of-the-art technology to digitally reconstruct the work, preserving the original format whilst repairing imperfections present in the aged copy. In rare cases, an imperfection in the original, such as a blemish or missing page, may be replicated in our edition. We do, however, repair the vast majority of imperfections successfully; any imperfections that remain are intentionally left to preserve the state of such historical works.

Forgotten Books is a registered trademark of FB &c Ltd.
Copyright © 2017 FB &c Ltd.
FB &c Ltd, Dalton House, 60 Windsor Avenue, London, SW19 2RR.
Company number 08720141. Registered in England and Wales.

For support please visit www.forgottenbooks.com

ANNUAL REPORT

—— OF THE ——

TOWN OF ALTON

FOR THE YEAR ENDING

FEBRUARY 15, 1895.

REPORTS

———OF THE———

SELECTMEN, TREASURER, CLERK, ROAD AGENTS, SCHOOL BOARD AND FIRE WARDS,

———OF THE———

TOWN OF ALTON,

———FOR THE———

FISCAL YEAR ENDING FEBRUARY 15,

1895.

LACONIA, N. H.:
PRESS OF WEEKS BROTHERS.
1895.

TOWN OFFICERS.

SELECTMEN.
JOSEPH A. MOONEY.
HERBERT J. JONES.
FRANK A. VARNEY.

TOWN CLERK.
GEORGE H. DEMERITT.

TREASURER.
LEWIS H. LAMPREY.

COLLECTOR OF TAXES.
ALVAH B. FLANDERS.

AUDITORS.
CHARLES D. MARSTON.
DAVID H. MORRISON.

SUPERVISORS.
BENJAMIN P. MARSTON.
DAVID E. CLOUGH.
OSCAR E. DAVIS.

SCHOOL BOARD.
OLIVER J. M. GILMAN.
SETH E. ROLLINS.
CHARLES H. McDUFFEE.

FIRE WARDS.
JOSEPH D. WILDER.
LABON G. WELCH.
FRED H. DOWNING.

POLICE.
DAVID E. CLOUGH.
JOHN M. BENNETT.

SELECTMEN'S REPORT.

VALUATION OF ALTON.

Real estate, No. of Acres, 35,605, value	$463,559.00
Personal estate, including polls	137,061.00
Total value	$600,620.00

	No.	Average.	Value.
Polls	414	$100.00	$41,400.00
Horses	448	59.96	26,865.00
Asses	2	25.00	50.00
Oxen	104	46.25	4,811.00
Cows	536	20.64	11,068.00
Neat Stock	190	15.86	3,015.00
Sheep	380	2.84	1,082.00
Hogs	9	9.44	85.00
Carriages	20	74.25	1,485.00
Stock in banks and other corporations			4,400.00
Money on hand and at interest			8,900.00
Stock in trade			21,400.00
Aqueducts			10,000.00
Mills and machinery			2,500.00
			$137,061.00

Total amount taxes raised		$12,973.39
State tax	$1,465.00	
County tax	2,251.37	
School tax	1,672.00	
Town tax	3,875.00	
Highway tax	2,101.55	
Percentage	246.55	
School house tax	1,351.00	
Percentage	10.92	
		$12,973.39

Tax on Poll money, $1.85.   Town School District tax, $0.31.

RECEIPTS INTO THE TREASURY.

1894.		Whole amount of taxes charged to collector	$12,973.39
Feb.	15.	Whole amount due from Collector Flanders	$2,326.05
	15.	Cash in treasury	43.90
Mar.	19.	Geo. E. Varney, by note ..	500.00
	20.	Alma C. Bennett, by note .	200.00
	20.	Sarah J. Clark, by note ..	100.00
	29.	Emily O. Emerson, by note .	250.00
	29.	Mary A. C. Evans, by note .	500.00
	29.	Frank D. Morse, by note .	1,100.00
	30.	Simeon Durgin, by note ..	1,500.00
April	7.	" " " ...	500.00
	18.	B. & M. Railroad, Seekins bill	18.00
	21.	Ella A. Gilman, by note ..	400.00
	27.	Caroline B. Davis, by note .	1,000.00
	28.	Fred R. Wadleigh, by note .	1,000.00
May	10.	John M. Bennett, hall rent .	10.00
	16.	H. J. Jones, license	3.00
	25.	Geo. H. Demeritt, dog license	130.80
	26.	Fred R. Wadleigh, by note .	500.00
	30.	Page D. Gooch, by note ...	100.00
June	2.	Fred S. Colbath, by note ..	200.00
	7.	Clarissa Chamberlin, by note	500.00
	19.	Edward Doane, by note ..	200.00
	19.	Emily O. Emerson, by note	100.00
Aug.	15.	Martha J. Sawyer, by note .	400.00
	15.	Isaac Morrill, by note ...	450.00
	16.	Hiram Edgerly, by note ..	140.00
	16.	S. Waldo Hurd, by note ..	200.00
Oct.	1.	Geo. H. Demeritt, dog license	77.62
Nov.	3.	H. J. Jones, hall rent ...	90.00
	3.	" license	2.00
	6.	Frank A. Varney, pauper ..	5.00
	6.	" " " .	9.00

Dec.	19.	State Treasurer, railroad tax	$627.12	
	19.	" " sav. bank tax	1,890.82	
	19.	" " literary fund	269.24	
	19.	" " b'nty, hawks	10.50	
1895.				
Jan.	15.	Co. of Belknap, pauper money	170.97	
Feb.	15.	H. J. Jones, hall rent . . .	7.00	
	15.	A. L. Rollins, fines . . .	35.62	
	15.	Esther A. Varney, note . .	225.00	
	15.	J. Jones, note	300.00	
				$16,091.64
				$29,065.03

EXPENDITURES.

Paid Weeks Brothers printing town reports	$45.50
American Express Co., books and express . .	3.05
G. H Demeritt, library	1.25
C. H. McDuffee, school supplies	87.37
S. E. Jones, decoration money	100.00
E. C. Eastman, books for town	13.50
C. H. McDuffee, school supplies	123.43
L. G. Welch, rent of library room	27.50
Ida E. Wells, water tub	3.00
P. H. Wheeler, return of births and deaths . .	10.25
C. W. Dore, water tub	3.00
D. H. Morrison, water tub	3.00
C. H. McDuffee, school supplies	39.58
J. M. Bennett, janitor	56.25
Geo. A. Rollins, water tub, '93 and '94	6.00
Jos. W. Howard, water tub, '92, '93, and '94 . .	9.00
J. D. Wilder, for fireman	137.46
State tax	1,465.00
County tax	2,251.37
	$4,509.26

MISCELLANEOUS BILLS.

Paid Moses Goodrich, curbing stone for hall	$150.00
H. P. Boody, assistance on camp ground	2.00
Samuel Morrison estate, winter work of '92 and '93	15.00
Tobias Berry, interest on notes	176.31
W. P. Emerson, printing ballots	12.50
Wolfeboro' Banking & Loan Co.	2,000.00
G. H. Proctor, extra work on vault	217.72
Gilbert & Baker Mfg. Co., gasoline	43.79
Mosler Safe & Lock Co., steel chest	75.00
L. G. Welch, for hose house	500.00
Susie A. Dore, note and interest	116.90
H. O. Mooney, curtains for hall	79.13
J. Haddock, repairs on road machine	21.05
S. E. Furber, work on vault	5.40
J. C. Flanders, work on vault	4.50
E. C. Morris, repairing vault	2.25
E. H. Rollins, extras on town hall	98.75
Clarissa Chamberlin, money on note	200.00
Horace E. Glidden, work on cellar	3.75
E. W. Chamberlin, work on cellar	2.25
S. E. Furber, work on cellar	9.00
Hiram W. Edgerly, money on note	15.00
J. C. Flanders, labor on cellar	10.24
F. W. Muzzey, labor on town hall	2.30
Morse & Varney, wood for library	5.00
G. E. Varney, note and interest	518.66
C. A. Bennett, building hose room	49.00
J. M. Bennett, coal for town hall	31.41
American Fire Hose Co., nozzle and bracketts	33.00
W. P. Emerson, printing	2.25
P. H. Wheeler, analysis of water	6.00
W. P. Emerson, stove for hose house	11.65
F. W. Muzzey, stove and furniture for hall	56.60
J. A. Mooney, wood for town hall	7.00
G. F. Savage heirs, land damage	25.00

Paid A. M. Kelley, land damage	$ 35.90
F. W. Muzzey, funnel for hose house	2.45
Oscar A. Garland, winter work '92 and '93	8.00
J. M. Bennett, lumber and labor	30.30
A. S. French, appraiser of dog damage	1.00
E. H. Rollins, appraiser of dog damage	1.00
A. L. Rollins, Eben Hayes, note and interest	320.00
Cogswell & Blackstone, attorney	21.25
H. J. Jones, insurance	50.00
Gilbert & Baker Mfg. Co., oil mixture	11.55
J. M. Bennett, labor	13.95
J. D. Wilder, repair on hose carriage	5.80
L. M. Rollins, teams	1.00
J. H. Fifield, teams	1.75
J. Jones & Son, supplies as per bill	267.30
Alton & Alton Bay Water Co., hydrants	746.25
" " " " " water rent and piping	39.31
Amos L. Rollins, insurance on town hall	50.00
H. J. Jones, hawks	2.00
" " express	1.00
F. A. Varney, hawks	5.00
" " printing and express	3.85
J. A. Mooney, car fare and expense	5.79
W. E. Sanborn, blacksmith	1.50
J. H. Fifield, bill for board	8.25
C. G. Drew, dog damage	3.00
C. V. Coffin, land damage	60.00
Geo. W. and J. M. Morrison, winter work '93	15.00
	$6,219.69

PAUPER BILLS.

Paid Moses Young, aid to George W. Gerrish	$5.00
Fred S. Bennett, aid to tramps	.50
H. F. Gilman, aid to Rosilla Blakely	3.50
D. E. Clough, tramps	8.40

ALTON TOWN REPORT.

Paid P. H. Wheeler, aid to L. Robinson family	$ 5.00
" " " John Joyce	21.75
" " " Moses Flanders	9.00
S. O. Wallingford, aid to Frank Clark	13.00
J. Jones, aid to F. Clark and G. Gerrish	16.50
The Downing Co., aid to J. D. Flanders	5.14
H. F. Gilman, aid to Rosilla Blakely	5.00
" " " " "	2.50
D. E. Clough, aid to tramps	13.05
P. H. Wheeler, aid to Mary Jones family	5.25
" " " Miss Williams	3.00
Morse & Varney, aid to J. D. Flanders	4.25
J. M. Bennett, aid to tramps	24.34
Patrick Lynch, aid to John Joyce	6.00
H. P. Evans, " " "	23.43
P. H. Wheeler, " " "	2.25
Annette P. Hanson, aid to C. H. Chamberlin family	22.00
Furber & Clark, aid to Ida T. Durgin	35.51
Geo. B. Clark, " " " "	27.50
J. M. Bennett, aid to tramps	3.82
L. M. Rollins, " "	4.00
J. Jones & Son, " "	4.50
H. J. Jones, " "	2.47
J. A. Mooney, overseer poor	6.00
J. H. Fifield, aid to tramps	2.25
D. E. Clough, " "	8.25
Willis E. Tetherly, aid to Ida F. Durgin	21.53
A. B. Lang, aid to Frank Clark	18.05
	$332.74
Dependent soldiers	$15.00
Paid treasurer town school district	$3,648.85
Paid treasurer of New Durham school district	3.16
Paid road agents, summer work	2,705.38
Paid road agents, winter work	1,444.56
Abatement of taxes	142.26

Paid building committee, hall $5,000.00
Paid building committee, hose house 500.00

TOWN OFFICERS' BILLS.

Paid S. W. Brown, ballot inspector	$2.00
Benjamin P. Marston, supervisor	7.00
Fred S. Bennett, police	2.00
D. E. Clough, supervisor	6.00
" " health officer	11.50
" " police	17.00
G. H. Demeritt, services as building committee	127.24
E. H. Rollins, " " "	96.57
C. H. Downing, " "	85.26
C. D. Marston, auditor	2.00
J. M. Bennett, police	21.00
D. E. Clough, supervisor	6.00
F. H. Carpenter, special police	21.00
B. P. Marston, supervisor	8.00
O. J. M. Gilman, police justice	3.00
E. H. Rollins, selectmen and inspector for '93	10.00
A. L. Rollins, " " " "	10.65
J. A. Mooney, " " " "	8.00
J. M. Bennett, police	3.00
" " licensing dogs	8.35
H. P. Horne, ballot inspector	2.00
Waldo C. Varney, ballot inspector	4.00
Harry P. Evans, " "	2.00
Oscar Duncan, " "	2.00
Joseph D. Wilder, fire ward	25.00
" " " services as committee on hose house	6.30
P. H. Wheeler, health officer	5.00
Frank Morse, services treasurer school district	25.00
Geo. II. Demeritt, services town clerk	73.10
Amos L. Rollins, police judge	70.00
T. H. Downing, committee hose house	5.00
" " fire ward	5.00

10 ALTON TOWN REPORT.

Paid H. J. Jones, selectman	$ 88.00
J. A. Mooney, selectman	88.00
" " recording inventory	15.00
F. A. Varney, selectman	86.00
O. J. M. Gilman, member school board	35.00
S. E. Rollins, " " "	35.00
C. H. McDuffee, " " "	40.00
A. B. Flanders, collector	175.00
L. H. Lamprey, treasurer	50.00
D. H. Morrison, auditor	7.50
C. D. Marston, auditor	7.50
D. E. Clough, police	25.00
L. G. Welch, fire ward and committee	10.00
J. F. Currier, supervisor	2.00
	$1,343.97

ABSTRACT OF RECEIPTS AND DISBURSEMENTS.

RECEIPTS.

Cash on hand Feb. 15, 1894	$ 43.90	
Total receipts during the year	25,361.77	
		$25,405.67

DISBURSEMENTS.

Total disbursements during the year	$25,364.88	
Cash on hand Feb. 15, 1895	40.79	
		$25,405.67

DEBT.

Liabilities Feb. 15, 1894	$13,367.39	
Assets Feb. 15, 1894	2,369.95	
Debt of the town Feb. 15, 1894		$10,997.44
Liabilities Feb. 15, 1895	$21,516 34	
Assets Feb. 15, 1895	3,772.45	
Debt of the town Feb. 15, 1895		$17,743.89
Increase of debt during year		$6,746.45

RECEIPTS.

Cash on hand Feb. 15, 1894	$ 43.90
Taxes from collector	11,640.08
Savings bank tax	1,890.82
Railroad tax	627.12
Literary fund	269.24
Bounty on hawks	10.50
County, for support of paupers	155.97
County, for support of dependent soldiers	15.00
Town notes	10,365.00
Dog licenses	208.42
Miscellaneous items	179.62
	$25,405.67

DISBURSEMENTS.

Town officers	$ 1,331.97
County paupers	248.20
Town paupers	84.54
Aid to dependent soldiers	15.00
Highways and bridges	2,705.38
Breaking roads	1,444.56
Damage by dogs	3.00
Support of schools	2,301.01
Repairs of school houses	1,351.00
School supplies	250.38
State tax	1,465.00
County tax	2,251.37
Fireman's tax	137.46
Memorial day appropriation	100.00
Committee on town hall	5,000.00
Committee on hose house	500.00
Town notes	2,915.00
Interest	431.88
Miscellaneous bills	2,829.13
	$25,364.88
Excess of receipts over disbursements	40.79
	$25,405.67

ASSETS.

Cash in hands of treasurer Feb, 15, 1895 . $	40.79	
Remaining in hands of collector Feb. 15, 1895	3,659.36	
Due from the county	72.30	
		$3,772.45

LIABILITIES.

Due sundry parties on town notes . . .	$21,041.68	
Due schools literary fund	269.24	
Due schools balance of dog license . .	205.42	
		$21,516.34
Indebtedness of the town		17,743.89

DOG LICENSES.

Cash received for dogs licensed . . . . $ 208.42

PAYMENTS.

Damage by dogs . . . . $	3.00	
Balance due schools	205.42	
		$208.42

Joseph A. Mooney,
Herbert J. Jones, } Selectmen of Alton.
Frank A. Varney,

We, the undersigned, having examined the foregoing account, find it properly vouched and correctly cast.

Charles D. Marston,
David H. Morrison, } Auditors

Alton, Feb. 15, 1895.

The foregoing report, containing a synopsis of the financial transactions for the past official year, we respectfully sudmit to the inhabitants of the town of Alton :

The increase of the debt, as will be seen, is $6,746.45, which is accounted for in various ways. Five thousand dollars of this was hired by vote of the town to complete the town hall. Two thousand dollars were raised to repair highways, but owing to the necessity of the cutting of bushes and the laying of sewer pipe, the appropriation was exceeded by $700. The cost of breaking roads in 1893 and '94 was $1,444.56. Paid for text books and school supplies, $250 ; expense of fitting up room for hose carriage, putting in vault, setting curbing and other necessary expenditures in and around the town hall amounted to about $1,000.

Town officers' bills exceed previous years owing to the extra committees chosen to superintend the building of town hall and hose house.

Many other extra bills, as will be seen by the report, have made our expenses unusually large.

Alton, Feb. 15, 1895.

JOSEPH A. MOONEY,
HERBERT J. JONES,
FRANK A. VARNEY,
Selectmen of Alton

REPORT OF CLERK OF POLICE COURT.

To the Selectmen of the Town of Alton:

I would most respectfully make the following report for money received since March 1, 1894, to date:

Cash received from fines	$10.00
" " for hearings	25.62
	$35.62

For which I would account for as follows:

Cash paid town treasurer of Alton $35.62

Amos L. Rollins, Clerk of Police Court.

TREASURER'S REPORT.

1894.

Mar.	19,	To balance of money in treasury . . .	$540.90
		To cash received of—	
Mar.	19,	H. J. Jones, selectman	500.00
	20,	" " "	300.00
	24,	A. B. Flanders, collector	60.00
	29,	F. A. Varney, selectman	1,100.00
	29,	H. J. Jones, "	750.00
	30,	J. A. Mooney, "	1,500.00
April	7,	H. J. Jones, "	500.00
	14,	A. B. Flanders, collector	143.00
	18,	H. J. Jones, selectman	18.00
	21,	" "	400.00
	27,	" "	1,000.00
	28,	A. B. Flanders, collector	120.00
	28,	H. J. Jones, selectman	1,000.00
May	10,	J. M. Bennett, for hall rent	10.00
	16,	A. B Flanders, collector	38.00
	16,	H. J. Jones, selectman	3.00
	25,	G. H. Demeritt, town clerk	130.00
	26,	H. J. Jones, selectman	500.00
	30,	J. A. Mooney, "	100.00
	31,	A. B. Flanders, collector	192.29
June	2,	H. J. Jones, selectman	200.00
	7,	F. A. Varney, "	500.00
	11,	A. B. Flanders, collector	141.05
	15,	" " "	275.00
	19,	H. J. Jones, selectman	300.00
	23,	A. B. Flanders, collector	150.00

June	30,	A. B. Flanders, collector	$ 133.28
July	7,	" " "	130.55
	14,	" "	73.13
	28,		73.00
Aug.	11,	" " "	138.02
	15,	H. J. Jones, selectman	850.00
	16,	" "	140.00
	16,	" "	200.00
	27,	A. B. Flanders, collector	370.00
Sept.	1,	" "	249.00
	22,	"	319.00
	29,	" "	203.00
Oct.	1,	G. H. Demeritt, town clerk	77.62
	13,	A. B. Flanders, collector	228.00
	20,	" "	301.00
	27,	" "	170.00
Nov.	3,	H. J. Jones, selectman, rent of town hall	90.00
	3,	" " for license	2.00
	3,	A. B. Flanders, collector	303.00
	6,	F. A. Varney, selectman	5.00
	8,	" "	9.00
	10,	A. B. Flanders, collector	482.00
	17,	" "	643.00
	24,	"	621.00
Dec.	1,	"	543.00
	8,		477.00
	15,	" "	421.00
	19,	J. A. Mooney, selectman, railroad tax	627.12
		Savings bank tax	1,890.82
		Literary fund	269.24
		Bounty on hawks	10.50
	22,	A. B. Flanders, collector	251.00
1895.			
Jan.	12,	A. B. Flanders, collector	906.00
	15,	J. A. Mooney, selectman	170.97
	19,	A. B. Flanders, collector	263.00
	26,	" "	230.00

Feb.	2,	A. B. Flanders, collector	$ 252.00
	11,	" "	327.00
	12,	" "	530.00
	15,	H. J. Jones, selectman, rent of town hall	7.00
	15,	A. B. Flanders, collector	419.00
	15,	" "	216.00
	15,	A. L. Rollins, fines of police court . .	35.62
	15,	A. B. Flanders, collector	215.00
	15,	" "	105.50
	15,	. . . . . .	175.00
	15,	" "	37.00
	15,	Joseph A. Mooney, selectman	525.00

$25,186.41

CASH PAID OUT.

(AS PER ORDERS.)

1894.

Mar.	19,	Paid E. H. Rollins	$500.00
	19,	" "	500.00
	26,	" "	300.00
	27,	H. J. Jones	3.05
	27,	" "	45.50
	27,	" "	5.00
	29,	E. H. Rollins	800.00
	29,	J. A. Cate	15.70
	29,	S. W. Brown	2.00
	30,	B. P. Marston	7.00
	31,	E. H. Rollins	1,000.00
	31,	Fred S. Bennett	2.50
April	7,	E. H. Rollins	150.00
	14,	Moses B. Goodrich	20.00
	14,	H. F. Gilman	3.50
	16,	Thomas Cogswell	15.00
	16,	G. H. Demeritt	200.00
	16,	H. P. Boody	2.00
	16,	E. H. Rollins	50.00

ALTON TOWN REPORT.

April	16,	Paid Tobias Berry	$ 176.31
	17,	C. V. Coffin	75.00
	17,	D. E. Clough	6.00
	21,	E. H. Rollins	50.00
	24,	" "	805.00
	28,	Moses B. Goodrich	50.00
	28,	W. P. Emerson	12.50
May	4,	E. H. Rollins	645.00
	9,	H. J. Jones	2,000.00
	10,	D. H. Morrison	50.00
	12,	Moses B. Goodrich	80.00
	19,	C. V. Coffin	25.00
	19,	Enos G. Rollins	50.00
	19,	David E. Clough	11.50
	26,	G. H. Proctor	217.72
	26,	G. H. Demeritt	125.00
	26,	S. E. Jones	100.00
	26,	L. G. Welch	150.00
	26,	Mosler Safe & Lock Co.	75.00
	26,	C. H. McDuffee	87.37
	26,	Gilbert & Barker Mfg Co.	43.79
	31,	E. H. Rollins	96.57
June	4,	Susie A. Dore	116.90
	6,	H. O. Mooney	79.13
	7,	G. H. Demeritt	127.24
	8,	C. H. Downing	85.26
	19,	Edson C. Eastman	13.50
	19,	J. Haddock	21.05
	19,	C. H. HcDuffee	123.43
	20,	Enos G. Rollins	100.00
	27,	Frank D. Morse	700.00
July	7,	G. W. Place	50.00
	9,	Enos G. Rollins	50.00
	23,	David E. Clough	8.40
Aug.	4,	G. W. Place	121.00
	14,	D. H. Morrison	250.00
	15,	L. G. Welch	350.00

ALTON TOWN REPORT. 19

Aug.	15,	Paid L. G. Welch . . . . $	27.50
	15,	Samuel E. Furber	5.40
	15,	John C. Flanders	4.50
	15,	E. C. Morris Safe Co.	2.25
	15,	E. H. Rollins	98.75
	16,	Clarissa Chamberlin	200.00
	25,	Enos G. Rollins	100.00
Sept.	1,	David E. Clough	17.00
	24,	Enos G. Rollins	50.00
Oct.	1,	M. M. Robinson, county treasurer	
		per receipt	1,000.00
	5,	John M. Bennett	21.00
	20,	P. H. Wheeler	35.75
	20,	S. O. Wallingford	13.00
	26,	The Downing Co.	5.14
	26,	F. W. Muzzey	2.30
Nov.	2,	John C. Flanders	10.24
	2,	Horace Glidden	3.75
	2,	C. D. Marston	2.00
	2,	Ernest Chamberlin	2.25
	2,	S. E. Furber	9.00
	2,	J. Jones & Son	16.50
	2,	H. W. Edgerly	15.00
	8,	G. E. Varney	518.66
	13,	C. A. Bennett	49.00
	13,	D. E. Clough	6.00
	13,	H. F. Gilman	5.00
	15,	C. H. McDuffee	29.16
	17,	Ida E. Wells	3.00
Dec.	4,	M. M. Robinson, county treasurer	
		per receipt	1,251.37
	8,	Enos G. Rollins	747.55
	8,	L. W. Rollins	10.00
	8,	P. H. Wheeler	6.00
	8,	Morse & Varney	5.00
	8,	John M. Bennett	31.41
	8,	G. W. Place	437.77

Dec.	12,	Paid C. V. Coffin	$ 353.96
	19,	Solon A. Carter, state tax per rc'pt	1,465.00
	22,	J. A. Mooney	7.00
	24,	F. D. Morse	1,000.00
	24,	W. P. Emerson	5.00
	24,	" "	2.25
	24,	" "	11.65
	28,	Frank W. Muzzey	56.60
	29,	G. W. Place	240.00
	31,	H. F. Gilman	2.50
1895			
Jan.	1,	David E. Clough	13.05
	3,	B. P. Marston	8.00
	12,	P. H. Wheeler	3.00
	12,	" "	10.25
	12,	" "	5.25
	12,	Morse & Varney	4.25
	12,	F. H. Carpenter	21.00
	12,	American Fire Hose Co.	33.00
	12,	Mrs. A. M. Kelley	35.00
	12,	J. M. Bennett	24.34
	12,	J. F. Currier	25.00
	19,	Frank D. Morse	500.00
Feb.	2,	D. H. Morrison	240.01
	2,	H. P. Evans	23.43
	2,	O. J. M. Gilman	3.00
	2,	Oscar J. Garland	8.00
	2,	P. H. Wheeler	2.25
	2,	Frank D. Morse	1,419.69
	2,	J. M. Bennett	30.30
	2,	D. H. Morrison	3.00
	9,	E. H. Rollins	10.00
	9,	C. H. McDuffee	39.58
	9,	Annette P. Hanson	22.00
	11,	E. H. Rollins	1.00
	11,	A. S. French	1.00
	11,	A. L. Rollins	320.01

ALTON TOWN REPORT. 21

Feb.	11,	Paid C. W. Dore ....$	3.00
	12,	F. W. Muzzey	2.45
	12,	Cogswell & Blackstone	21.25
	12,	Furber & Clark	35.51
	12,	H. J. Jones	50.00
	12,	Gilbert & Barker	11.50
	12,	Patrick Lynch	6.00
	12,	F. P. McDuffee	391.42
	14,	John M. Bennett	85.37
	15,	Lorin M. Rollins	5.00
	15,	Frank D. Morse	25.00
	15,	G. A. Rollins	6.00
	15,	W. C. Varney	4.00
	15,	P. C. Ham	3.16
	15,	Oscar Duncan	2.00
	15,	H. P. Evans	2.00
	15,	J. D. Wilder	174.56
	15,	P. H. Wheeler	5.00
	15,	J. W. Howard	9.00
	15,	Alton & Alton Bay Water Co. ...	785.56
	15,	L. G. Welch	10.00
	15,	H. P. Horne	2.00
	15,	G. B. Clark	27.50
	15,	G. H. Demeritt	73.10
	15,	D. H. Morrison	3.00
	15,	A. L. Rollins	50.00
	15,	" "	80.65
	15,	W. E. Sanborn	1.50
	15,	F. H. Downing	10.00
	15,	G. H. Fifield	1.75
	15,	J. A. Mooney	122.79
	15,	A. B. Flanders	175.00
	15,	O. J. M. Gilman	35.00
	15,	John H. Fifield	10.50
	15,	C. H. McDuffee	40.00
	15,	F. A. Varney	94.85
	15,	Seth E. Rollins	35.00

Feb.	15,	Paid D. C. Clough	$ 8.25
	15,	" "	25.00
	15,	C. V. Coffin	150.16
	15,	" "	60.78
	15,	C. D. Marston	7.50
	15,	D. H. Morrison	7.50
	15,	G. W. Place	588.59
	15,	H. J. Jones	93.47
	15,	J. Jones & Son	271.83
	15,	A. B. Lang	18.05
	15,	W. E. Tetherly	21.53
	15,	C. G. Drew	3.00
	15,	L. H. Lamprey	50.00

$25,145.62

Cash received $25,186.41
Cash paid out 25,145.62

Cash in treasury $40.79

LEWIS H. LAMPREY, Treasurer.

We, the undersigned, having examined the foregoing account, find it properly vouched and correctly cast.

D. H. MORRISON, } Auditors.
C. D. MARSTON,

Alton, Feb. 15, 1895.

ROAD AGENT ACCOUNT.

REPORT OF C. V. COFFIN.

Road Agent for the Winter of 1893 and 1894.

CASH RECEIVED.

1894.			
April 17.	To cash of selectmen	. . . . $	75.00
May 19.	" "	. . . .	25.00
Dec. 12.	"	. . . .	353.96
1895.			
Feb. 12.	"	. . . .	150.16
Feb. 15.	"	. . . .	60.78
			$664.90

CASH PAID OUT.

Paid C. F. Hayes . . . . $	13.80
J. D. Flanders	6.00
A. Ellis	4.50
J. C. Young	3.15
A. N. Young	1.80
Albert Ellis	18.75
G. W. Horn	6.03
Mrs. Frank Coffin	7.16
A. B. Flanders	14.05
W. F. Webber	.75
H. A. Ellis	6.45
R. B. Yeaton	.75
W. A. Burnabee	3.85
Samuel Stockbridge	.45
George Nute	11.85
S. E. P. Gilman	42.60

Paid B. Frohock	$ 6.00
S. E. Batchelder	2.26
H. B. Ricker	2.33
S. E. Rollins	11.13
Calvin Rollins	18.98
S. E. Furber	.30
J. A. Mooney	.45
C. F. Brooks	3.44
Luther Place	41.25
G. R. Prescott	12.85
B. P. Marston	9.45
B. F. Frohock	23.85
Danna Morse	6.34
Cyrus Harriman	3.90
F. S. Gilman	8.18
L. E. Avery	12.23
C. B. Dore	3.94
J. M. Gilman	27.43
C. S. Glidden	5.00
David Lamprey	18.00
J. B. Ham	.45
O. D. Glidden	12.45
H. H. Flanders	7.65
L. Colbath	6.00
M. M. Flanders	1.80
M. R. Place	3.00
I. B. Bennett	3.00
W. H. Rollins	.98
J. Weeks	.52
G. A. Rollins	4.81
Isaac Straw	1.05
P. D. Gooch	1.35
F. L. Gilman	.75
S. B. Flanders	9.15
Charles Hayes	5.55
I. Gilman	3.00
John Nutter	9.50

Paid C. V. Coffin	$ 41.55
George Rudd	2.55
W. S. Watson	4.80
A. J. Gilman	22.65
Jones & Lamprey	.30
Moses Young	1.20
Charles Clough	.38
Frank Glidden	3.30
Horace Glidden	7.43
R. B. Yeaton	.75
A. J. Brown	1.65
T. H. Cass	6.30
D. Parnell	6.25
I. B. Gilman	3.15
J. L. Blakely	1.50
L. G. Paige	14.73
C. H. Flanders	8.43
I. B. Gilman	35.85
John Leavitt	4.05
C. D. Marston	6.97
C. Perkins	2.83
A. Ellis	11.70
H. Flanders	.52
George Place	41.00
Charles Emerson	2.50
Bert Young	1.50
G. F. Emerson	.30
John Bennett	.50
	$664.90
Cash received	$664.90
Cash paid out	664.90

C. V. Coffin, Road Agent.

We, the undersigned, having examined the foregoing account, find it correctly cast.

C. D. Marston, } Auditors.
D. H. Morrison, }

Alton, Feb. 15, 1895.

REPORT OF FRANK P. MCDUFFEE.

For winter work of 1893 and 1894.

CASH RECEIVED.

1895.
Feb. 11, Received of Selectmen . . . . $ 391.42

CASH PAID OUT.

Paid Frank P. McDuffee	$50.00
Lewis H. Proctor	14.55
James W. Goodall	8.97
Charles F. Rand	8.72
Edwin O. Prescott	14.55
R. W. Price	2.70
John Crockett	.53
Chas. L. Pinkham	2.70
Dana Bradley	4.05
H. J. Pinkham	2.85
Horace S. Wells	7.65
Frank A. Prescott	3.00
Jacob F. Evans	5.40
David H. Morrison	40.00
Simeon Durgin	1.85
John L. Gerrish	2.70
A. B. Lang	17.00
Geo. W. Colbath	4.00
Chas. Tebbetts	13.50
Edmund Stone	13.20
Chas. Hayes	8.10
Chas. Drew	8.00
James Woodman	5.40
Otis Wallingford	.38
Frank Furber	13.30
Sylvester B. Huckins	9.17
Charendon Chamberlin	10.55
B. F. Furber	10.00

Paid Eben Hanson	$ 15.75
John F. Hanson	14.85
Joseph E. Berry	6.53
W. H. Berry	4.36
Daniel Watson	6.30
J. Morrison	10.00
Joseph W. Howard	23.00
Frank W. Howard	14.56
M. S. H. Kimball	12.50
Warren E. Bradley	.75

$391.42

We, the undersigned, having examined the foregoing account, find it correctly cast.

C. D. MARSTON, } Auditors.
D. H. MORRISON, }

Alton, Feb. 15, 1895.

REPORT OF ENOS G. ROLLINS.
For Winter Work of 1893 and 1894.

CASH RECEIVED.

1894.
Mar. 29.	Received of selectmen	$	15.70
May 19.	" "		50.00
July 9.	"		50.00
Dec 8.	"		272.54

$388.24

CASH PAID OUT.

Paid C. C. Mooney	$ 14.97
William Hayes	9.38
Ezekiel Hayes	16.46
J. W. Durgin	.72
S. D. Watson	1.50
H. J. McDuffee	5.18
S. D. Hurd	3.37
Seth C. Walker	7.43

Paid S. E. Roberts	$ 15.50	
Stephen Shagnon	12.00	
Herbert E. Morrill	4.00	
Clarence Morrill	1.95	
Fred Morrill	1.50	
H. C. Tuttle	7.50	
E. G. Rollins	96.70	
Albert Varney	25.50	
E. Hodgdon	18.95	
		$388.24

We, the undersigned, having examined the foregoing account, find it correctly cast.

C. D. MARSTON, } Auditors.
D. H. MORRISON, }

Alton, Feb. 15, 1895.

REPORT OF ENOS G. ROLLINS.

For Summer Work of 1893 and 1894.

CASH RECEIVED.

1894.

June 20,	Received of selectmen	$ 100.00	
Aug. 25,	" "	100.00	
Sept. 24.	"	50.00	
Dec. 8.	"	475.01	
			$ 725.01

CASH PAID OUT.

Paid Arthur Cate	$ 9.00
Milton Greenleaf	15.00
John Johnson	39.00
Alfred Lucas	23.25
John Dustin	18.00
Charles Rines	3.00
Joseph Hoyt	28.50

Paid Frank Getchell	$ 12.00
Warren Nutter	34.00
George Rollins	10.50
Stephen Shagnon	32.90
George Cate	24.00
M. Merrow	2.50
John H. Evans	9.00
Charles Whitehouse	1.20
Charles Rines	8.62
Samuel Gerry	5.25
J. A. Cate	15.70
A. E. Lucas	4.42
J. McDuffee's heirs	15.83
J. Q. Adams	4.80
A. J. Varney	6.04
Albert Woodman	3.98
Oran French	.50
Hiram Wallingford	3.30
David S. Lougee	6.98
R. B. Hurd	16.50
John Berry	3.41
I. W. Springfield	5.00
Frank Carpenter	12.00
Henry Story	4.00
Albert Carter	2.70
Chester Twombly	2.25
Sumner Cotton	11.65
Edson Roberts	29.10
Loami Dore	23.47
Charles Whitehouse	12.45
Romeyn Hurd	19.95
Stephen Watson	1.50
John Berry	7.65
Charles McDuffee	10.88
Fred Woodman	6.30
Alonzo Berry	10.50
Albert Woodman	3.00

Paid Henry Woodman	$ 3.00	
Charles Nutter	31.50	
John Evans	1.50	
Andrew Varney	5.25	
Sumner Cotton	3.00	
Percy Walker	3.68	
Seth C. Walker	5.47	
Chester Twombly	2.70	
A. J. Varney	4.80	
Albert Varney	19.95	
Charles Mooney	3.46	
E. G. Rollins	266.75	
		$725.01

We, the undersigned, having examined the foregoing account, find it correctly cast.

C. D. MARSTON, } Auditors.
D. H. MORRISON,

Alton, Feb. 15, 1895.

REPORT OF G. W. PLACE.

CASH RECEIVED.

1894.
July 7,	To cash received	$50.00
Aug. 4,	" " "	121.00
Dec. 4,	" " "	437.77
Dec. 29,	" " "	240.00
Feb. 15,	" " "	588.59
		$1,437.36

CASH PAID OUT.

Paid C. V. Coffin	$327.62
Jones & Lamprey	5.10
John J. Nutter	3.82
J. O. Gleason	9.42

ALTON TOWN REPORT.

Paid S. J. Rollins	$ 6.00
I. G. Felker	8.25
H. A. Ellis	16.65
J. B. Ham	1.50
Horace Glidden	37.05
Charles Parnell	33.00
Don Parnell	61.20
George Gerrish	29.50
R. B. Yenton	42.95
George Dore	7.35
G. W. Berry	32.25
Lyonia Colbath	86.25
Seth D. Hurd	7.50
J. Collins	4.50
C. D. Marston	5.62
Charles Hayes	3.00
Irad Gilman	28.65
Moses Flanders	10.12
Charles Hill	4.35
John L. Weeks	2.25
Alfred G. Ellis	26.85
Lewis Avery	3.00
John Gilman	9.10
B. L. Perkins	.60
Ira Bennett	1.50
Joseph A. Mooney	4.50
O. J. M. Gilman	1.50
Dr. A. H. Hayes	4.00
Ben P. Marston	2.75
Luther Place	13.52
Frank Glidden	11.70
Wm. McIntire	3.00
Dana Morse	2.25
Hamilton Reynolds	1.50
Julien Emerson	9.00
Frank Davis	9.60
S. O. Wallingford	40.75
Timothy Ricker	3.00

Paid Andrew J. Gilman	$ 1.50
Calvin Rollins	1.50
Harrison Ricker	3.00
C. H. Downing & Co.	1.53
Wm. Watson	1.50
Jonathan Blakely	2.70
Geo. Colbath	3.75
John M. Bennett	4.50
Calvin Flanders	6.94
Gilman Paige	7.87
Woodbury Rollins	6.00
David Lamper	3.00
Irad Gilman	6.00
Orren Glidden	10.00
Hiram Flanders	6.85
Ai Gilman	15.15
Clark Perkins	1.50
John G. M. Jones	5.22
Jones & Place, 32 loads grade	3.20
Orren Glidden	7.20
Eri Warner	5.00
Calvin Rollins	4.50
S. E. Rollins	5.10
C. W. Rollins	2.10
Harrison Ricker	5.55
Timothy Ricker	5.25
Alvah Flanders	11.26
C. H. Flanders	1.20
S. E. Batchelder	3.75
Albert Ellis	6.00
A. J. Gilman	10.50
S. E. Furber	3.00
Wm. S. Watson	5.50
G. W. Place	198.90
Will Dore	2.85
S. E. P. Gilman	121.00
S. J. Rollins	3.00
O. J. M. Gilman	3.75

Paid John M. Gilman . . . . $ 18.22

$1,437.36

Cash received $1,437.36
Cash paid out 1,437.36

GEORGE W. PLACE, Road Agent.

We, the undersigned, having examined the foregoing account, find it properly vouched and correctly cast.

CHARLES D. MARSTON, } Auditors
DAVID H. MORRISON,

Alton, Feb. 15, 1895.

REPORT OF DAVID H. MORRISON.

CASH RECEIVED.

1894.
May 10, Received of selectmen . . . . $ 50.00
July 14,   "   " 250.00
1895.
Feb. 2,   " 240.01
Feb. 15, ...   3.00
                                         ——— $543.01

CASH PAID OUT.

Paid David H. Morrison . . . . $ 164.68
    David A. Morrison 33.50
    James N. Morrison 24.02
    Joseph W. Howard 25.52
    James W. M. Kimball 1.50
    Shurburn S. Wells 27.02
    Luther Kimball 10.12
    Frank W. Howard 24.82
    William H. Berry 1.50
    Joseph E. Berry 2.25
    Eben Hanson 3.00

Paid John Hanson	$ 3.00	
Samuel Deland	6.00	
Charles Rand	13.95	
Charles G. Drew	73.00	
Benjamin F. Furber	1.50	
Ira C. Chamberlin	7.95	
Sylvester B. Huckins	2.25	
Lyman Berry	6.75	
James Goodall	17.98	
Charles L. Pinkham	6.82	
Andrew Pinkham	10.95	
John Crockett	5.55	
James Woodman	14.85	
Fred Davis	6.00	
Frank P. McDuffee	9.00	
Lewis A. Proctor	5.25	
Frank Furber	10.50	
Charles Hayes	6.00	
Daniel Watson	7.32	
Hiram E. King	1.50	
Henry R. Wentworth	1.09	
Eugene F. Goodwin	2.00	
Dana Bradley	1.87	
Moses Young	4.00	
		$543.01
Cash received		$543.01
Cash paid out		543.01

DAVID H. MORRISON, Road Agent.

We, the undersigned, having examined the foregoing account, find it correctly cast.

C. D. MARSTON, } Auditors.
D. H. MORRISON,

Alton, Feb. 15, 1895.

REPORT OF BUILDING COMMITTEE.

The Building Committee respectfully submits the following report :

CASH RECEIVED.

1893.		
June 3.	Received from town treasurer	$ 200.00
Aug. 11.	" " " "	500.00
Aug. 24.	" " " "	1,000.00
Aug. 30.	" " " "	600.00
Sept. 2.	" " " "	400.00
Sept. 9.	" " " "	300.00
Sept. 15.	" " " "	300.00
Sept. 23.	" " " "	400.00
Sept. 30.	" " " "	400.00
Oct. 7.	" " "	200.00
Oct. 11.	" " " "	100.00
Oct. 14.	" " " "	350.00
Oct. 20.	" " "	300.00
Oct. 25.	" " " "	914.25
Oct. 27.	" " " "	550.00
Nov. 7.	" " "	350.00
Nov. 17.	" " " "	222.00
Dec. 9.	" " " "	220.00
1894.		
Jan. 10.	" " "	1,343.75
Mar. 19.	" " " "	500.00
Mar. 19.	" " " "	500.00
Mar. 26.	" " "	300.00
Mar. 29.	" " " "	800.00
Mar. 31.	" " " "	1,000.00
April 7.	" " " "	150.00

April 13.	Received from town treasurer	$	200.00
April 16.	" " " "		50.00
April 21.	" " " "		50.00
April 24.	" " "		805.00
May 4.	" " " "		645.00
Received from town treasurer for lot			1,350.00
" " selectmen for vault			540.00
			$15,540.00

CASH PAID OUT.

1893.

Aug. 14.	Paid G. H. Proctor & Son	$	500.00
Aug. 30.	" " "		600.00
Sept. 1.	" "		1,000.00
Sept. 2.			400.00
Sept. 9.	"		300.00
Sept. 16.	"		300.00
Sept. 23.	"		400.00
Sept. 30.	"		400.00
Oct. 7.	"		300.00
Oct. 11.	"		350.00
Oct. 20.	"		300.00
Oct. 25.	"		914.25
Oct. 27.	"		550.00
Nov. 7.	"		350.00
Nov. 17.	" " "		762.00
Dec. 4.	George W. Place		174.45
Dec. 9.	G. H. Proctor & Son		220.00
Dec. 29.	" " "		620.00
Dec. 30.	Amos L. Rollins		52.50

1894.

Jan. 10.	A. Moulton & Co.		427.00
Jan. 10.	Thayer & Fletcher		100.00
Jan. 12.	G. H. Proctor & Son		100.00
Jan. 20.	E. H. Rollins		15.00
Feb. 3.	Freight		.41
Feb. 10.	G. H. Proctor & Son		535.00

Feb. 13.	Paid American Express	$	.15
Feb. 26.	G. H. Proctor & Son		140.00
Feb. 28.	Littifield & Ferry		18.00
March 1.	G. H. Proctor & Son		5.00
March 14.	Laconia Lumber Co.		26.90
March 20.	F. G. Durgin		233.00
March 22.	Charles A. Mellen		8.75
March 22.	B. L. Blaisdell		76.00
March 22.	C. H. Downing & Co.		20.49
Macrh 22.	G. H. Proctor & Son		913.00
March 23.	Freight		.25
March 23.	J. Jones & Son		2.27
March 28.	G. H. Proctor & Son		50.00
March 29.	John M. Bennett		6.50
March 30.	G. H. Proctor & Son		750.00
April 7.	" " "		163.00
April 7.	J. F. Flanders		4.50
April 9.	Freight		.42
April 10.	"		1.66
April 11.	American Express		3.15
April 12.	Freight		5.29
April 13.	"		.36
April 14.	"		1.26
April 14.	Andrew Demarest Seating Co.		500.00
April 16.	Express		.15
April 17.	"		3.00
April 19.	Freight		.47
April 19.	"		5.04
April 20.	G. H. Proctor & Son		50.00
April 20.	Freight		.32
April 21.	Express		.65
April 23.	Laconia Lumber Co.		144.25
April 23.	L. J. Couch & Co.		210.00
April 24.	C. L. Jenness		6.90
April 25.	Edd & Hurd		7.20
April 25.	F. P. Hayes		6.90
April 26.	Express		.15

April	27.	Paid M. W. Twombly . . . . $	8.61
April	28.	Freight	.63
April	30.	"	3.02
May	1.	W. E. Sanborn	.75
May	1.	L. M. Hall	115.00
May	2.	Express	.35
May	2.	Rochester foundry	7.67
May	3.	F. G. Durgin	46.99
May	4.	Express	.30
May	5.	George Dore	1.65
May	5.	Charles Hill & Son	1.80
May	5.	Moody Parnell	.45
May	5.	Gilbert Barker & Co.	390.00
May	5.	" " "	173.20
May	5,	Freight	2.13
May	5.	A. T. Ramsdell	295.00
May	5.	G. H. Proctor & Son	51.25
May	5.	G. H. Fifield	6.75
May	5.	J. H. Seavey	23.16
Feb.	9.	Wolfboro' Loan and Banking Co .	15.00
April	15.	Jones & Lamprey	.60
May	5.	Mooney & Varney	4.05
May	5.	J. Jones & Son	9.26
May	5.	Gilbert Barker & Co.	35.00
May	5.	Laconia Lumber Co.	60.54
Cost of lot			1,350.00

Cr. By cash paid $15,638.75
Dr. To cash received from town 15,540.00

Balance due building committee $98.75

We, the undersigned, having examined the foregoing account, find it properly vouched and correctly cast.

D. H. MORRISON, } Auditors.
C. D. MARSTON, }

Alton, May 22, 1894.

SCHOOL REPORT.

The School Board have the honor to submit for your consideration their annual report for the school year ending Feb. 15, 1895. There have been thirty-three terms of school during the year, taught by fifteen different teachers, one male and fourteen females. Whole number of different scholars registered, 230; number that studied arithmetic, 169; algebra, 19; geography, 128; grammar, 98; physiology, 47; history, 52; bookkeeping, 13; composition, 62; drawing, 30; penmanship, 220; reading and spelling, 230.

School No. 1. South Alton.

Summer term, taught by Helen P. Tucker. Whole number of scholars, 9; average attendance, 8. Fall and winter terms taught by Velzora Deland. Whole number of scholars, 9; average attendance, 9.

School No. 2. Lang's Corner.

Summer term taught by Lillie M. Bickford. Whole number of scholars, 11; average attendance, 10. Fall and winter terms taught by Bertha L. Jones. Whole number of scholars, 14; average attendance, 13.

School No. 3. Village.

Walter H. Miller had charge of the grammar school. Whole number of scholars registered for the first term, 26; average attendance, 24; second term, 21; average attendance, 19; third term, 17; average attendance, 13. Primary department has been under the instruction of Carrie E. Morse. Whole number of scholars registered, 41; average attendance, 39.

School No. 4. Gore.

Three terms of school, each taught by Bertha L. Boynton. Whole number of scholars, 11; average attendance, 10.

School No. 5. McDuffee.

Three terms of school, taught by Lena B. Shaw. Whole number of scholars, 17; average attendance, 17.

School No. 6. Gilman's Corner.

Two terms of school, both taught by Julia A. Tuttle. Whole number of scholars, 11; average attendance, 10.

School No. 7. East Alton.

Two terms of school, each taught by Abbie E. Cate. Whole number of scholars, 17; average attendance, 16.

School No. 8. Bay.

Carrie E. Jones, teacher. Whole number of scholars registered, 35; average attendance, 33.

School No. 9. Loon Cove.

This school has been under the instruction of Luella Crockett. Whole number of scholars, 4; average attendance, 4.

School No. 10. West Alton.

Sadie M. Kelley had charge of the summer term and Mabel F. Kelley taught the fall and winter terms. Whole number of scholars, 7; average attendance, 6.

School No. 11. Mountain.

Edith V. French, teacher. Number of scholars registered, 18; average attendance, 16.

With a few exceptions, the scholars in all our schools have manifested a good interest in their studies, and have made commendable progress. Our teachers have generally been faithful, competent and true to the best interest and advancement of their pupils. We regret to say, however, that during the past year, as in former years, there has been a lack of interest on the part of parents in the village. In the grammar school we find there are more or less scholars who leave school for some trifling cause and are often sustained by their parents. It has been a common practice for boys and girls in this school, as soon as they are old enough to earn a little money to leave school and go into the shop, making the great mistake that the acquisition of knowledge is of less value than money. It would seem that parents, knowing the advantages of an education, would prize it so highly as to be unwilling to have their children stay out of school a single day. After the town has made liberal appropriations for its schools, and the school board has furnished a competent teacher, it is a serious wrong for parents to allow their children to remain away from school when not absolutely necessary. Some are agitating the subject of appropriating larger sums of money for the support of schools, but we believe it would be far wiser to help form a public opinion that will make a better use of what we now appropriate. There are many things that we want in our schools, but our greatest want is punctual and constant attendance of children. If we wish to have our boys and girls become useful and honored members of society and be successful in life let us not cut short their school days by allowing them to leave school at the early age that many of them do at the present day. We leave this subject to the careful consideration of parents. The most of our teachers attended the teachers' institute held at Laconia and also the one held at Farmington. We would urge every teacher to avail themselves of these opportunities. These institutes are designed for the benefit of teachers, a place where they may meet and discuss new methods of instruction, and where they will hear some of the most learned and able educators of the state speak upon important matters relating to their interests, and it would seem strange indeed if any teacher could not gain some useful ideas by being present and taking part in the meetings. The registers of the year have been carefully kept, and we find in most of the schools there has been a general improvement as regards the attendance, cases of absence and tardiness being much less frequent than last year. Four hundred and nine visits have been made by parents and citizens during the year. This is the largest number that we have ever been enabled to report, being nearly one hundred in excess of last year. These visits give pleasure and encouragement to both teacher and pupil.

Having long felt that our scholars needed more study on the meaning of words we have bought twelve copies of Webster's dictionary and placed them in the hands of the teachers. It has also been thought best, after consulting with our teachers, that during the coming year a change should be made in our readers, as they have been in use so long the scholars have become tired of reading the same pieces over so many times. We are pleased to observe that many of our scholars are excellent writers. This has been brought about in some of the schools by teachers training their pupils to write as they learn to read. We are glad to state also that in most of the schools when visited the last day we have listened to many fine exercises, consisting of declamations, essays and select readings. The importance of compositions and declamations in the way of forming habits of correct writing and speaking, and in teaching fluency and confidence in the expression of ideas, cannot be overestimated.

There have been ten schools that have had each twenty-eight weeks of school and two schools that have had twenty-four weeks of school each the past year. Miss Cate of the East Alton school resigned her position as teacher some four weeks before the time for the term to finish, and as it was so late in the season and liable to be bad traveling, it was thought best by most of the parents to have the rest of the term kept out in the spring. Miss Kelley, on account of sickness, did not finish the winter term by four weeks at West Alton.

We are now able to report that all the school houses in town are in a good condition. The East Alton and Gilman's Corner school house, and the Loon Cove school house have peen thoroughly remodeled and put in excellent condition, and we consider them a credit to the town. Each of these houses have been furnished with new single desks and chairs. The repairs and furnishings have all been done at a cost not exceeding the appropriation. The annual school meeting will be held Saturday, March 16, 1895, at 2 o'clock p. m., and it is hoped that all voters interested in the educational interests of the town will be present. Respectfully submitted.

OLIVER J. M. GILMAN,) School Board
SETH E. ROLLINS,   }   of
C. H. McDUFFEE,   )   Alton.

ROLL OF HONOR.

EAST ALTON.—Maud Whitehouse, 2 terms; Percy Getchel, 2 terms; Arthur Getchel, 1 term; Nelson Rines, 1 term.

BAY.—Harry S. Downing, 2 terms; Stephen Lynch, 1 term; Edgar Glidden, 1 term; George Lynch, 1 term; John Hurly, 1 term; Lena Chamberlin, 1 term; Annie M. Hurly, 2 terms; Carroll T. Jones, 1 term; Mabel Jones, 1 term; Cora B. Jones, 1 term; Maud Jones, 1 term; Eva Varney, 1 term.

LOON COVE.—Welcome C. Jones, 2 terms; Herbert F. Webber, 1 term.

WEST ALTON.—Wesley Hatch, 2 terms; Haven Rollins, 1 term; Seth E. Batchelder, 1 term.

MOUNTAIN.—Frank E. Davis, 2 terms; Willie S. Davis, 3 terms; Cynthia J. Davis, 3 terms; Frank W. Marston, 1 term; Walter N. Marshall, 2 terms; Charles D. Nutter, 1 term; Cora E. Nutter, 1 term; Sadie E. M. Gilman, 1 term; Charlie D. Lamprey, 1 term; Ersmus W. Ellis, 1 term.

SOUTH ALTON.—Mary G. Berry, 2 terms; Philip R. Berry, 2 terms; Gertrude Berry, 1 term; Elsie R. Deland, 2 terms; Will E. Furber, 1 term.

LANG'S CORNER.—Effie M. Prescott, 2 terms; Mabel Smith, 1 term.

GORE.—Addie M. Glidden, 2 terms.

GILMAN'S CORNER.—Roscoe W. Cotton, 2 terms; Arthur C. Cotton, 2 terms; Grace B. Berry, 1 term; Ernest A. Hurd, 1 term.

VILLAGE.—(Grammar)Ruth M. Clough, 2 terms; Henry W. Nutter, 1 term; Edna P. Peabody, 2 terms; Grace L. Rudd, 2 terms; Annie A. Wheeler, 1 term; Clarence C. Woodman, 2 terms; George H. Young, 2 times; Mattie C. Peabody, 1 term; Nellie S. Place, 1 term; Ambie E. Tilton, 1 term. Primary department. Cassie Perkins, 1 term; John P. Hurd, 1 term; Clifton J. Flanders, 1 term; Leona Parnell, 2 terms; Pearl S. Bassett, 1 term; Gracie G. Blaisdell, 1 term; Winnie E. Carpenter, 1 term; Bernice A. Currier, 1 term; Nora A. Parnell, 1 term; Addie S. Flanders, 1 term; Eddie W. Coffin, 1 term.

McDUFFEE.—A. A. Barr, 2 terms; Mabel Woodman, 1 term; Henrietta Woodman, 1 term.

RECEIPTS AND EXPENDITURES OF THE ALTON SCHOOL DISTRICT FOR 1894.

RECEIPTS.

Balance in hands of District Treasurer, March 1, 1895	$250.99
Raised by tax for support of schools	1,668.84
" for repairs	1,000.00
Literary fund	280.85
Railroad tax	100.00
Dog tax and license	248.16
District debts	336.00
Insurance	15.00
	$3,899.84

EXPENSES.

Paid teachers' salaries and board	$2,205.75
District debts	343.46
Fuel and fitting the same	93.03
Miscellaneous expenses	72.67
Repairs	1,049.73
	$3,764.64

Balance on hand, Feb. 15, 1895 . . $135.20

INDEBTEDNESS OF SCHOOL DISTRICT.

Notes due 1895, on account of Bay school house	$300.00
Notes due 1896, on account of Bay school house	300.00
Interest to Feb. 15, 1895	110.00
	$710.00

OLIVER J. M. GILMAN, } School Board
SETH E. ROLLINS, } of
C. H. McDUFFEE, } Alton.

We, the undersigned, having examined the foregoing account, find it correctly cast.

C. D. MARSTON, } Auditors.
D. H. MORRISON, }

Alton, Feb. 15, 1895.

School District Treasurer's Report.

CASH RECEIVED.

1894.
March 31.	To balance of money in treasury . . . $	250.99
June 27.	Received of L. H. Lamprey	700.00
Nov. 16.	" " "	29.16
Dec. 24.	"	1,000.00

1895.
Jan. 19.	"	500.00
Feb. 2.	" " "	1,419.69

$3,899.84

CASH PAID OUT.

1894.
April 14.	Paid Hiram O. Tuttle . . . . $	4.40
25.	A. L. Rollins	15.00
30.	F. D. Morse	3.75
May 26.	J. Jones & Son	2.07
26.	F. M. Ayer	2.00
26.	W. R. Musgrove	.75
26.	E. C. Eastman	3.10
29.	Stephen Shannon	1.00
June 27.	Luella Crockett	72.00
28.	Helen P. Tucker	54.00
28.	Lena B. Shaw	66.00
28.	Carrie E. Jones	70.00
29.	Sadie M. Kelley	60.00
29.	Edith V. French	77.00
30.	Carrie E. Morse	85.00
30.	Lillie M. Bickford	72.00

ALTON TOWN REPORT.

June	30.	Paid Bertha L. Boynton . . . . $	72.00
	30.	Walter H. Miller	100.00
	30.	Abbie E. Cate	72.00
July	2.	Julia A. Tuttle	60.00
Sept.	26.	Moses Goodrich	2.50
	29.	Mrs. Oscar Davis	2.00
Oct.	6.	A. J. Gilman	1.25
	18.	Lewis Blaisdell	4.50
Nov.	16.	J. L. Haurenett	29.16
Dec.	24.	Julia A. Tuttle	80.00
	25.	Velzora A. Dealand	60.00
1895.			
Jan.	4.	Dana B. Morse	10.00
	4.	Edith V. French	119.00
	4.	B. L. Blaisdell	14.00
	7.	Bertha Jones	96.00
	7.	Joseph Watson	1.75
	8.	Lena B. Shaw	102.00
	12.	Luella Crockett	96.00
	15.	Orin Glidden	.60
	17.	Bertha L. Boynton	96.00
	18.	Willie P. Emerson	1.50
	18.	Seth 'E. Grant	6.00
	18.	Carrie E. Morse	153.00
	18.	Mabel F. Kelley	42.00
	18.	Frank D. Morse	6.00
	18.	Mable F. Kelly	54.00
	19.	Walter H. Miller	191.25
	19.	Carrie Jones	130.50
	19.	Frank Furber	3.00
	21.	Frank Muzzy	2.50
	21.	Joseph A. Cate	2.50
	21.	R. B. Hurd	4.00
	21.	Charles Jones	.50
	21.	Julia Jones	4.50
	21.	Herman O. Tuttle	11.75
	21.	David E. Clough	4.92

48 ALTON TOWN REPORT.

Jan.	21.	Paid Abbie E. Cate	$ 72.00
	23.	George Chamberlin	1.00
	23.	G. W. Place	10.00
Feb.	2.	Fred S. Gilman	8.25
	2.	John Hurd	2.00
	2.	C. H. McDuffee	18.90
	2.	J. A. Mooney	7.00
	2.	S. E. Rollins	11.50
	2.	Velzora A. Dealand	63.15
	2.	J. Jones & Son	15.30
	2.	C. H. McDuffee	14.75
	2.	Charles A. Bennett	7.50
	2.	Town of Barnstead	13.50
	2.	Frank D. Morse	5.00
	2.	B. L. Blaisdell	2.25
	4.	Manitowoc Seating Co.	184.10
	4.	O. J. M. Gilman	31.10
	4.	Moses Goodrich	40.00
	4.	H. O. Tuttle	363.75
	4.	Charles A. Bennett	191.85
	4.	Albert Woodman	2.00
	4.	C. H. Downing	1.48
	4.	W. A. Burnaby	130.00
	4.	Lucy J. Horn	212.00
	4.	Alonzo French	131.00

Cash received $3,899.84
Cash paid out 3,764.64

Cash in treasury $135.20

FRANK D. MORSE, Treasurer.

We, the undersigned, having examined the foregoing account, find it properly vouched and correctly cast.

C. D. MARSTON, } Auditors.
D. H. MORRISON, }

Alton, Feb. 15, 1895.

LIBRARY REPORT.

To the Selectmen of Alton:

Gentlemen—The Library Trustees respectfully submit, through you, a few items of interest concerning the library for the consideration of the people of Alton.

On March 18th, 1892, the town voted to accept the gift of the state of one hundred dollars' worth of books. and voted to raise the sum of fifty dollars. in order to receive the gift of the state, and elected Geo. H. Demeritt, John F. Currier, Waldo C. Varney, trustees.

The library was opened to the public on Dec. 31, 1892, in temporary quarters over Labon G. Welch's drug store, with one hundred volumes, the gift of the state.

The amount raised by the town was expended as follows:

Received from selectmen		$50.00
Paid Geo. W. Libby for books	$49.25	
Freight on books	.65	
Cartage on books	.10	
		$50.00

March 1893, the town voted to raise the sum of one hundred dollars, and was expended as follows:

Received of selectmen		$100.00
Paid Judson, Marsh & Co. for books . . .	$97.50	
" " " record book . .	1.50	
Freight on books	.65	
Rubber stamp	.35	
		$100.00

March 18, 1894, the town voted to raise the sum of one hundred and twenty-five dollars, and was expended as follows:

Received of selectmen $125.00
Paid DeWolf, Fisk & Co., for books . . . $125.00

$125.00

The Alton Free Public Library was moved into the library and reading rooms in the new town hall, June 9, 1894, and is pleasantly located, but at that time needed some extra furniture, and through the efforts of the trustees and the Alton Dramatic club, of which the trustees are members. The following articles were presented the library: A large mantel with plate glass, the cost of which was $65.00, brass furniture and rail for fire place at a cost of $20,00, a brass guard rail in front of book case, the cost of which was $25.00.

We have caused to be printed catalogues containing all the books that were in the library at that time, at a cost of $35.00. We have only sold thirty of them at 25 cents each, making $7.50, leaving the library in debt $27.50, also $8.00 for printing cards, rules and slips, making the debt of $35.50, this was from money in the hands of treasurer of the dramatic club.

We wish to extend our thanks to the other members of the dramatic club for their assistance, and also to Miss Lena Carpenter, Miss Ruth Clough, Miss Ella Fifield and Miss Carrie E. Moses, who have assisted as librarians without pay.

We also wish to thank Mrs. Otis Hinwand for her gift of 96 volumes of Atlantic Monthly, from 1886 to 1893; 144 volumes of Century Magazines, from 1882 to 1893; 12 volumes Scribner's Monthly, from 1881; 144 volumes Harper's Magazines, from 1881 to 1893, which are unbound. The trustees wish the town to appropriate at the coming town meeting $65.00 for binding the same.

The following persons have given books, for which we wish to thank: Mrs. Geo. Craine, Geo. S. Bassett, H. G. Clough, James M. Jones, Mooney & Varney, Rosie Estes, Chester A. Twombly, Mrs. John M. Gilman, Lafayette Woodman, Richard B. Yeaton.

Whole number books in library is 743, number of books loaned, from Feb. 15, 1894 to Feb. 15, 1895, was 6,002, requiring the handling of 12,004 books.

The business of the library is steadily increasing, as the journal of the library will show, and unless the appropriation of the town is increased the patrons will soon be obliged to read the same books over again or look elsewhere for their reading matter. Respectfully submitted.

GEO. H. DEMERITT,
JOHN H. CURRIER, } Trustees.
WALDO C. VARNEY,

Births Registered in the Town of Alton for the Year Ending December 31, 1894.

Name of Child [if any.]	Male	Female	Living or Stillborn.	No. Child, 1st, 2d &c.	Color.	Name of Father.	Maiden Name of Mother.	Color.	Residence of Parents.	Occupation of Father.	Birthplace of Father.	Birthplace of Mother.	Age of Father.	Age of Mother.
11 Jessie Mable		F	Living	5		Samuel J. Glidden	Mable Mitchell		Alton	Shoemaker	Alton	Alton	25	30
	M		"	1		Lewis Robinson	Ethel Varney		"	Laborer	Fall River, Mass.	"	29	24
9		"	Stillborn	3		Charles H. Rines	Alice Ryan		"	Shoemaker	New Durham	Nova Scotia	34	24
27		"	Living	4		George E. Furber	Ada Hunter		"	Farmer	Alton	Barnstead	32	29
3 Lucindy		"	"	2		John K. Jones	Carrie B. Lowell		"	"	"	Hiriam, Me.	42	23
25		"	"	1		Willis E. Glidden	Jennie E. Buzzell		"	Shoemaker	"	Alton	27	21
	"		Stillborn	1		Samuel W. Brown	Frances Nourse		"	Clerk	"	Lynn, Mass.	28	31
7		"	Living	1		Page D. Gooch	Emma J. Pinkham		"	Farmer	"	Alton	44	40
10	"		"	1		Willis E. Sanborn	Electa A. Furber		"	Blacksmith	Gilmanton	"	27	25
2		"	"	1		Ernest F. Brown	Ida M. Gray		"	Shoemaker	"	Sandwich.	New Durham.	28	28
21 Walter Maxfield	"		"	1		William G. Crafts	Florence A. Crafts		"	Painter	Taunton, Mass.	Dover, Me.	48	15
4		"	"	2		Darias S. Harriman	Etta B. Lamper		"	Shoemaker	Eaton	Alton	21	20
12	"		"	1		Osman R. Furber	Annie E. Coffin		"	Clerk	Alton	"	38	30
30		"	"	2		James C. Emerson	Annie H. Hanson	All White	"	Clergyman	Barnstead	Barnstead	35	22
5 Lester F.	"		"	1		Fred H. Downing	Minnie I. Barr	All White	"	Merchant	Alton	Weymouth, N. S.	28	24
13	"		"	3		Robert A. Frohock	Fannie A. Whitehouse		"	Farmer	Gilford	Alton	50	46
20		"	"	4		Chester A Twombly	Marietta Varney		"	"	"	"	32	13
30		"	"	1		Moses W. Twombly	Nellie M. Sanders		"	Mechanic	Gloucester, Mass	Moultonborough	21	24
14 Lena Evelyn		"	"	2		Fred E. Varney	Matilda Vickery		"	Conductor	Tuftonboro'	Gilford	32	23
18	"		"	1		Charles I. Buzzell	Addie B. Hatch		"	Farmer	Rochester	Somersworth	34	28
25 Evelyn Gengla		"	"	1		Edward S. Clark.	Lizzie M. Varney		"	Engineer	Alton	Alton	27	26
22	"		"	1		George S. Chamberlin	N. Maud Hurd		"	Farmer		Boston. Mass.		
1 Minnie		"	"	7		Merille Adams	Emma Wallingford		"	Woodchopper	Canada	Canada	39	22
1 Carrie Estilla		"	"	3		John Tardy	Delia Bufford		"	Shoemaker	Alton	Chichester	24	18
11 James Henry	"		"	1		George B. Recker	Dora S. Leaver		"	Farmer	"	Ireland	41	36
12		"	"	4		James W. Goodell	Anne Grimes		"	"	"	Alton	36	27
31		"	"	1		Charles H. W. Jones	Tena G. Thompson		"	"	"	"	35	19
						Orrin A. Lamper	Grace A. Hayes							

Marriages Registered in the Town of Alton for the Year Ending December 31, 1894.

Place of Marriage.	Name and Surname of Groom and Bride.	Residence of each at time of Marriage.	Age of each.	Color of each.	Occupation of Groom and Bride.	Place of Birth of each.	Names of Parents.	Birthplace of Parents.	Occupation.	What Marriage, 1st, 2d, &c.	Name, Residence, and Official Station of Person by whom Married.
1 New Durham	Willie M. Stevens	Alton	22		Shoemaker	Alton	Martin B. Stevens	Alton	Farmer	1st	Rev. C. D. Crockett, New Durh'm
	Carrie P. Fletcher	"	27		Housekeeper	Danvers, Mass.	Mary M. Stevens	"	Housekeeper		
							Jacob Berry	Deceased	Deceased		
28 Alton	Enos B. Whitehouse	Troy, Vt.	51		Carpenter	Alton	Eliz'beth Berry	Alton	Housekeeper	2d	Rev. J. C. Osgood, Alton.
	Sarah A. Chamberlin	Alton	50		Housekeeper	Middleton	Daniel Whitehouse	"	Deceased		
							B. L. Tufts	Canada			
8 Alton	George B. Ricker	"	24		Shoemaker	New Durham	David Tufts	Middleton	Farmer	1st	Rev. N. Glidden.
	Dora S. Leaver	Epsom	17		Housekeeper	Epsom	George W. Ricker	Alton	Farmer		
							Abbie M. Ricker	"	Housekeeper		
							Frank Leaver	Epsom	Painter		
							Martha Leaver	"	Housekeeper		
26 Wolfeboro'	Herbert E. Morrill	Alton	32		Farmer	Alton	Wm. H. Morrill	Tuftonborough	Farmer	1st	Rev. Wm. K. Lucas, Wolfeboro
	Mattie A. Shaneon	"	17		Housekeeper	"	Susan Morrill	"	Housekeeper		
							Stephen Shaneon	Canada	Housekeeper		
							Nettie Shaneon	"	Hou ekeeper		
19 Farmington	George A. Dore	"	20		Shoemaker	"	Alvin A. Dore	"	Shoemaker	1st	Rev. S. H. Goodwin, Farm'ton.
	Hattie Watson	"	16		Shoe Stitcher	"	Flora L. Dore	Canada	Housekeeper		
							Joba S. Watson	Alton	Housekeeper		
							Jessie Watson	"	Housekeeper		
15 Alton.	Benjamin P. Berry	"	26	All White	Painter	Holderness	Samuel B. Berry	Holderness	Farmer	1st	Rev. J. C. Emerson Alton.
	Grace M. Taylor	"	20	All White	Shoe Stitcher	Alton	Emma E. Berry	"	Housekeeper	2d	
							Amos L. Rollins	Alton	Farmer		
	John Allen	"	34		Farmer	Canada		Deceased	Deceased		
12 Middleton	Sadie Wiser	Middleton	29		Housekeeper	"	John Allen	"		2d	David E. Frost, J. P., Middlet'n
							Sarah Allen	"			
	Frank A. Prescott	Alton	25		Farmer	Alton	Frank Berry	Unknown	Unknown	1st	Rev. J. G. Mungey, Gilmanton.
16 Barnstead	Lunna M. Hurd	Barnstead	24		Housekeeper	Barnstead	Flora E. Prescott	Boston. Mass.	Housekeeper		
							A. C. Hurd	Barnstead	Farmer		
							Mary D. Hurd	"	Housekeeper		
7 Alton.	Iri W. Mitchell	Alton	55		Farmer	New Durham	Samuel Mitchell	Deceased	Deceased	3d	Geo. H. Demeritt, J. P., Alton
	Ruth A. Newell	"	43		Housekeeper	Bradford Co. Pa	Sally Mitchell	"			
							Edward C. Dewing	"			
							Susan A. Dewing				
9 Alton	James H. Kennie	"	23		Laborer	Westbrook, Me	James H. Kennie	New Brunswick	Farmer	1st	Rev. J. C. Osgood, Alton
	Bessie Parnell	"	17		Shoe Stitcher	Canada	Alsea Kennie	"	De eased		
							Charles Parnell	Canada	Housekeeper		
21 Gilmanton	Clarence L. Andrews	Westbro'k Me	23		Laborer	Westbrook, Me	Martha Parnell	Concord			
	Eva Wallingford	Alton	17		Housekeeper	Alton	Franklin P. Andrews	Eastport, Me	Fireman	1st	Rev. E. T. Hurd, Gilmanton.
							Laura L. Andrews	N. Hampshire	Housekeeper		
							Otis Wallingford	Alton			
							Betsey Wallingford	"	Housekeeper		
8 Wolfeboro'	George W. Rollins	"	27		Farmer	"	Enos G. Rollins	"	Farmer	1st	Rev. T. S. Weeks, Wolfeboro-
	Flossie A. Brown	"	20		Housekeeper	"	Adeline Rollins	"	Deceased		
							Andrew R. Brown	Maine			
							Abbie Brown	Alton	Deceased		
18 Laconia	Irad B. Gilman	"	49		Farmer	"	Manach G. W. Gilman			2d	Rev. F. S. Beckford Laconia.
	Nellie M. Gray	Sanbornton	40		Housekeeper	Lakeport	Mercy Gilman	Gilford	Housekeeper		
							Joseph B. Mudgett	Meredith	Farmer		
							Olive J. Mudgett	"	Deceased		
24 Gilmanton	Everett W. Emerson	Alton	29		Shoemaker	Alton	Abbut S. Emerson	Alton	Shoemaker	1st	Rev. E. T. Hurd, Gilmanton.
	L. Maud Page	Gilmanton	23		Shoe Stitcher	Gilmanton	Ann E. Emerson	Barnstead	Housekeeper		
							Edwin J. Page	Sandwich	Carpenter		
							Addie L. Page	Gilmanton	Housekeeper		

Ending December 31, 1894.

		Sex	Color.	Single, Mar'd, or Widowed	Occupation.	Place of Birth. Father.	Place of Birth. Mother.	Name of Father.	Maiden Name of Mother.	Disease or Cause of Death.
10	Clara J. Colbath	28		7 10	New Durham	F	M	Housekeeper	Alton	Middleton	Elihu Hayes	Sarah E. Hayes	Consumption
28	Charles G. Hayes			6 15	Alton	M	S		New Durham	Moultonboro	James H. Hayes	Etta	Stoppage
	Rines								Nova Scotia		Charles H. Rines	Alice M. Ryan	"
6	Sally Chamberlin	78	9	16	Strafford	F	W	Housekeeper	Unknown	Ireland	William Sloper	Hannah Brown	Old Age
23	Timothy Donovan	73	7	2	Ireland	M		Railroad man	Ireland	Ireland	Dennis T. Donovan	Elizabeth Goodwin	"
4	Sarah A. Twombly	72	2	3	East Wakefield	F		Housekeeper	ParsonsField	Newfield	John Dore	Mary Hanson	Paralysis
23	Benjamin Jones	76	1	1	Strafford	M		Farmer					Old Age
5	George T. Leeds	72	5		Dorchester, Ms.	M		Carpenter			Charles Leeds	Elizabeth Tilestone	Cancer
19	Martha Varney	76			Meredith	F		Housekeeper	Deerfield	Deerfield	William Lane	Irville Crane	Paralysis
21	Sarah M. Clogston	53			Unknown	F	M		Hopkinton	Hopkinton	Rodney Brown	Abigail Esty	Heart Disease
4	Henry C. Badger	62			New York	M	W				Joseph Badger	Sterling	Heart Disease
15	Ozius Goodrich	60	10	24	Worth'gton, Ms	M		Clergyman	Connecticut	Connecticut	Warren Goodrich	Ann Bowers	Apoplexy
10	Cordelia J. Flanders	15	7	27	Gilford	F			Ca vin H. Flanders	Loulla B. Sawyer	Consumption
19	Joshua Varney	90	11	10	Rochester	M		Cabinet makr	Rochester	Great Falls	Thomas Varney	Sarah Tebbetts	Old Age
23	Chas. F. Stockbridge	46	3	6	Alton	M		Jeweler	Alton	Jackson	Isaac Stockbridge	Mehitable Lucy	Consumption
6	Andrew Huckins	74	5	17	Madbury	M		Farmer	Madbury	Barrington	John B. Huckins	Abigail Moses	Accident
7	Phoebe R. Coffin	79	1	1	Gilmanton	F		Housekeeper	Gilmanton	Gilmanton	Nehemiah Clough	Sarah Clough	Diabetes
16	Anna A. Kicker	59	5	13	Alton	F			Alton	Middleton	John Rollins	Mary Perkins	Chronic Hepatitis
23	Mary W. Lucus	89	4	8	Alton	F			Somersworth	Brookfield	Moses Willey	Susan Whitehouse	Old Age
2	Not named		2	19	Alton				Gilford	Alton	Robert A. Frohock	Fannie Whitehouse	"
8	Benj. Whitehouse	68	5	11	"	M		Farmer	Middleton	Acton	Enos Whitehouse	Betsey Trickey	Diabetes

I hereby certify that the above return is correct, according to the best of my knowledge and belief. GEORGE H. DEMERITT, Town Clerk.